The Adventures of
Clarissa and Gregory

Nadine Redfield
Illustrated by
Nadine Redfield and Macaeli J. Pickens

© Nadine Redfield, 2017. All rights reserved. No part of this work may be scanned, copied, uploaded or reproduced in any form or by any means, graphically, electronically or mechanically, without written permission from the copyright holder.

ISBN: 978-1-943492-27-5 (hard back)

ISBN: 978-1-943492-28-2 (soft cover)

Book design by: designpanache

www.elmgrovepublishing.com
San Antonio, Texas

This book is dedicated to my daughter,
Dawn Redfield Olbrich,
who's idea it was to write these stories down!

Contents

Meet Clarissa and Gregory..7

Clarissa's First Wagon Ride...9

The Handkerchief Doll...13

Clarissa Cuts Off Her Curls...17

Clarissa and Gregory Move to the Country.............................20

Clarissa Gathers the Eggs..24

How to Make a Handkerchief Doll.......................................29

*Clarissa and Gregory.
Clayton, Michigan, 1929*

Meet Clarissa and Gregory

Clarissa and Gregory are real children, a brother and sister who lived in America a long time ago, long before there were cell phones or computers or even television.

They had lots of adventures together!

They still talk about their adventures and now they would like to share their stories with you.

Some of their adventures are very funny. And some of them are very scary!

Clarissa and Gregory hope you enjoy finding out what it was like to grow up in America many years ago. It wasn't so different to today, really.

Although they didn't have cell phones and computers, they did have lots of other toys. Like a red wagon that went very, very fast. And a doll made from a handkerchief.

At the end of the book, Clarissa will show you how to make one!

The Adventures of
Clarissa and Gregory

Clarissa's First Wagon Ride

In the year 1929 Clarissa lived in the small village of Clayton, Michigan. One warm summer day, her mother was doing the family washing.

"Look at that big bubble, Mama!" Clarissa said. She poked the bubble with her finger then giggled when it disappeared.

"This is a lovely summer day. A nice breeze is blowing. So the clothes will dry nicely when I hang them on the line," Mama told her.

Mama reached into the round wash tub, pulled out a wet sock, laid it across the scrub board, and rubbed it with a cake of P&G laundry soap. P&G stood for Proctor and Gamble Co. that made soap. Clarissa listened to the hollow rub-a-dub sound her mother made when she rubbed a sock on the ridges of the square washboard to get it clean.

BANG! Went the screen door as Gregory, Clarissa's four-year-old brother, ran into the kitchen, his mop of blond hair hanging over his

The Adventures of Clarissa and Gregory

forehead. He had let the screen door slam behind him.

"Gregory, please don't let the screen door slam behind you next time," Mama reminded him.

"Mama, may I take Clarissa for a ride in my new red wagon?"

"I guess you can if you're careful. She has never ridden in your wagon before." Mama took a comb and combed Clarissa's light brown ringlets so she would look nice for the wagon ride.

"Come on, let's go!" Gregory ordered as he grabbed Clarissa's hand and led her outside to his parked wagon on the sidewalk.

Clarissa climbed in the back of the wagon watching Gregory put his right leg in the wagon and his right hand on the handle to steer. Then with the other hand he hung on to the side of the wagon. The left leg was on the sidewalk ready to push off.

Gregory made a humming sound, pretending he had a motor, to get the wagon in motion. The little couple traveled down the sidewalk on Elm Street. A huge elm tree grew along the sidewalk, shading the children from the sun. Gregory spotted some wood chips along the sidewalk.

"I am going to gather up some of these chips for kindling. Mama will need them to start a fire in her cook stove tonight."

Clarissa watched him gather the chips and lay them in the wagon beside her.

"Ouch, they hurt my leg," Clarissa complained, pushing the chips away to the front of the wagon.

"That will be enough to start a fire tonight."

"Can we go over there and play?" Clarissa asked, pointing to the children playing by the sidewalk around the corner.

The Adventures of Clarissa and Gregory

"Okay," Gregory answered as he turned the corner, racing as fast as he could. "The wagon rides better with you in the back, and it's nice to have someone to talk to."

As the wagon drove closer to the children playing in the grass, a big boy thought it would be fun to take Gregory's wagon away with his little sister in it. Well, the big bully was in for a surprise. When he grabbed the handle out of Gregory's hand to pull the wagon away, Gregory reached down and picked up one of the wood chips and threw it at the boy. It hit him over his right eye. Blood streamed down his face. The boy screamed and ran home as fast as his legs could carry him. Clarissa felt sorry for the

"The wagon rides better with you in the back, and it's nice to have someone to talk to."

The Adventures of Clarissa and Gregory

boy who was hurt, even though he had done wrong.

Gregory and Clarissa raced home. "Gregory, slow down! I almost fell out of the wagon. You are going too fast!"

Gregory explained to their mother what had happened. Mama talked to the boy's mother on the phone. The mothers made peace. The bully knew he had done wrong.

"Clarissa, why are you crying?" Mama asked.

"I didn't get to play with the children."

"We'll go for another ride tomorrow. We can play with them then," Gregory told her.

Clarissa looked forward to another ride in the wagon. She felt safe having a brave brother to protect her.

A few days later, Mama, Gregory and Clarissa visited the injured boy. Clarissa looked at the small red scar over his eye. She didn't think he looked like a big bully anymore.

Never again did he try to take away Gregory's red wagon with Clarissa in it.

Clarissa looked at the small red scar over his eye.

The Handkerchief Doll

    Clarissa loved to go to church and Sunday School on Sundays and hear Bible Stores about Jesus. In church she looked at the ladies' hats and the pretty flowers lined up across the platform in front of the podium.

    Saturday evening, everyone took a bath in a round corrugated wash-tub. They went to bed early and got up in the morning to dress for church. Daddy put his overalls aside then got out his Sunday suit, put on his black dress shoes, a white shirt and a colorful necktie. He put on his Sunday hat when he was ready to go. Mama wore her best dress, high heels and a fancy hat. She never went to church or to town without a hat. It usually sat on top of her head and it never could keep her head warm. Clarissa wandered why she always wore a hat.

    Gregory wore his Sunday best pants and shirt with a necktie smaller than Daddy's. Daddy always tied his tie for him, because Gregory didn't know how to make a knot in a necktie yet. Mama helped Clarissa dress

The Adventures of Clarissa and Gregory

in a nice clean dress that she had made for her. The little family walked down the sidewalk listening to the church bells ringing loudly. This announced that it was time to come to church and worship.

When they reached the church they climbed the steep steps up to a room called a vestibule, where the men took their hats off and hung them on hooks lined up along one wall. A long rope hung down that was used to ring the church bell. Through the door was the sanctuary with pews where the people sat. The pews faced a stage where the preacher stood and the choir sang.

The beautiful flowers lined up across the front of the stage were roses, daffodils, lilacs, daisies and tulips.

The Adventures of Clarissa and Gregory

A stairway descended down to the basement where the children attended Sunday School classes. Clarissa loved to listen to Aunt Nellie tell stories about Jesus. Aunt Nellie used Bible figures that she cut out of card and colored. She stood the figures in a sand box and moved them around while telling the stories. The children sat on little red chairs around the sand box. Clarissa loved the story about Jesus feeding thousands of people with a little boy's lunch of 2 loaves and 3 fishes. The children also learned a simple Bible verse like "God is love" to recite to the big folks upstairs.

When church started, the family sat in a pew together. The beautiful flowers lined up across the front of the stage were roses, daffodils, lilacs, daisies and tulips. There might be some big round peonies of white, red, or pink. Clarissa watched the ladies with colorful fans that they swung back and forth to keep cool. She listened to the songs, but when the minister started to preach, Clarissa became restless trying to understand the big words.

Mama reached into her purse and pulled out a clean handkerchief that she had folded and twisted into a little doll for Clarissa to play with. Sometimes Mama took a pencil and drew two eyes on the face of the doll. Clarissa sat quietly through the service playing with the doll.

Sometimes Mama made two dolls for Clarissa to play with if she had two clean handkerchiefs.

When church was over, the dolls were taken apart and put back into Mama's purse, in case she sneezed or had a tear to wipe away if she heard a sad story.

Clarissa pictured herself all grown up with a purse full of hankies and a fancy hat on her head. She never dreamed there would ever be anything like tissues in her purse when she grew up.

Learn how to make a handkerchief doll of your own! Turn to the back of the book for a, easy-to-follow step-by-step diagram. All you need is a handkerchief or any piece of fabric at least 6 inches square.

Clarissa Cuts Off Her Curls

It was a nice warm summer day. Clarissa and Gregory were playing outside, running around and in and out of a large tent someone had put up to dry. When they grew tired of playing in the tent, Clarissa thought of something else to do.

"Gregory will you go inside and get my little scissors with green handles." Clarissa asked her brother.

The scissors were given to them at the Bible School they attended a week ago. Gregory found the little scissors with green handles and handed them to Clarissa.

"What are you going to do with the scissors?" Gregory asked.

Clarissa didn't answer. Instead she began cutting off her curls. She handed the curls to Gregory. He carried them outside and hid them under the tent flap.

The Adventures of Clarissa and Gregory

Pretty soon Clarissa had cut off all her curls.

The Adventures of Clarissa and Gregory

Snip, snip. She handed more curls for him to hide.

"Why do you want to cut your hair, Clarissa?" Gregory asked.

"It hurts when Mama combs my hair, and I don't like it when everyone makes a fuss over my curls," Clarissa told her brother. She wanted folks to talk to her – not talk about her long curls, and play with them. "There is a little girl under here," she thought.

Pretty soon Clarissa had cut off all her curls. Mama suddenly appeared with a horrified look on her face.

"Clarissa, what have you done?" Mama asked, disappointed to see her little girl without any curls.

"I used my little green scissors to cut my hair," Clarissa replied.

"You had better come on in the house and I'll trim your hair so it won't look so ragged," Mama said.

Clarissa never was sorry she had cut off her curls, even though she was now just a "Little Plain Jane." No longer did folks make a fuss over her curls. Nor did it hurt when Mama combed her hair!

Clarissa and Gregory Move to the Country

When Clarissa was around four-years-old, she moved with her family to the country into a rent house. It was across from Daddy's saw-mill at the edge of the woods.

Mama told the children, "Some day we'll build our own bungalow, with an upstairs, over there across the road. Your grandmother gave us the land where Daddy has his saw mill at the edge of the woods."

It was different living in the country. Clarissa was a little sad to leave the village with sidewalks. She loved playing on the sidewalks and watching the neighborhood children play. On the sidewalk she could do so many things, like play hopscotch, or roller-skate, ride a tricycle (if you were luck enough to own one), bounce a ball, roll a tire, ride a wagon or push a doll buggy or carriage. Not that Clarissa had done any of these things, but she dreamed she would, when she was old enough.

The Adventures of Clarissa and Gregory

"Mama, come look at the red flower I found in the front yard!"

The Adventures of Clarissa and Gregory

Now her only playmate was her brother and he went with Daddy on errands a lot. Gregory was old enough to go to school. Mama thought that her two children needed to live in the country to grow up. Clarissa made the most of living in the country. She enjoyed helping her Mama feed the chickens. She played with her baby doll named Pauline and Tommy, the family's black cat.

Grandmother lived about a mile away with Uncle Ray, who was a bachelor. He stayed on the farm to take care of his mother. Most of his brothers and sisters had married and moved to farms of their own. It was fun to walk down the road to visit Grandmother. If it was a nice day they could walk through the woods and across the meadow where the cows grazed.

One day Clarissa was lonely. She was wandering around the yard when she saw something red growing inside a circle of old wire fence. She walked closer and saw a beautiful red flower with a black center. It was the most beautiful flower she had ever seen. She ran inside to tell, Mama, about it.

"Mama, come look at the red flower I found in the front yard!" Clarissa called, out of breath. Mama stopped her ironing and came outside to see the flower.

"It is a red poppy. Someone planted it and it made seeds so it could grow up by itself. Yes, it is beautiful. Look at the black center, and at the round buds on the stems. They will make more flowers later." Mama explained.

"I will look for more flowers tomorrow."

Another day Clarissa went to visit the school with her brother.

The Adventures of Clarissa and Gregory

They walked down the gravel road just a little way from their house. It was a one-room schoolhouse built on a hill. She entered through the door into a small room called a coat room where the children hung their coats and hats, and left their boots when it was cold and snow covered the ground.

Inside the large room there were rows of desks with the seats attached. The children in the school were all ages. They attended classes from the first to the eighth grade.

One big girl handed Clarissa a tin of watercolors with a brush, some paper and a glass full of water. The kind girl showed Clarissa how to put the brush in the water, then in the little squares of paint and paint on the paper. This is a lot more fun than coloring with crayons, she thought. She wanted to do this again. She thought the transparent colors were brilliant, and she fell in love with painting with watercolors.

Now living in the country, Clarissa got to walk through the woods and pick wild flowers.

Daddy even made maple syrup in early spring at the Sugar Bush, deep in the woods beyond the creek. The Sugar Bush was a building with a cubicle on the roof to let out the steam while the sap was boiling to make maple syrup. It was fun visiting Daddy and watching him make maple syrup. He drove his big steam engine into the woods to make steam that went through pipes that boiled the sap from the maple trees that made the syrup. At the end of the day, after all the half gallon tins were filled, there was some was left over, so they brought it home to pour over their pancakes for breakfast the next morning.

Clarissa decided that living in the country wasn't so bad after all.

Clarissa Gathers the Eggs

Mama bought some hens so they could have their own eggs. The hens lived in a chicken coop, sometimes called a hen-house, with a big rooster. The hens ran loose during the day, but at night they slept in the coop. The chicken coop had boxes attached to the wall across the front of the building where the hens laid their eggs. Yellow straw lined the square boxes to make them nice and soft. This kept the eggs from breaking. The coop protected the hens from wild animals such as skunks and raccoons that roam during the night looking for food. The animals try to steal the eggs and eat them.

It was fun to watch the hens and rooster during the day. The rooster called the hens when he found a tasty morsel of food such as a juicy worm, an insect or a piece of grain. The hens came running and the one that got there first got the treat. Sometimes the rooster ate the treat

The Adventures of Clarissa and Gregory

himself, but most of the time he enjoyed feeding his ladies because it made him feel important.

Once in a while a hen decided she wanted to have some baby chicks. She went off to herself and made a nest away from the chicken coop where she laid her eggs. She sat on the eggs for 24 days to keep them warm, so the little chicks inside the eggs would grow. It was always a surprise when the mother hen appeared from hiding with a trail of baby chicks parading behind her. The baby chicks were soft and fluffy, They were usually yellow but sometimes they were black or brown. Clarissa loved to catch a little fuzzy chick and hold it. It snuggled up and closed its eyes and made a peep-peep sound to let her know it was happy. Clarissa thought they were the cutest things ever.

The Adventures of Clarissa and Gregory

When the mother hen found some food she called her babies to come eat the bits of food. When it was time for a nap or night-time, the mother hen fluffed her feathers up so the baby chicks could run underneath her and keep warm. If the mother hen thought her babies were in danger, or if it started to rain, she would call them, and they ran safely under her feathers out of the rain.

One morning Mama was so busy she didn't have time to collect the eggs. She decided Clarissa was old enough to gather eggs.

"Clarissa, would you take this basket, and gather the eggs for me? I am very busy today canning peaches. When you pick up the eggs be careful not to squeeze them too tight or they will break. We keep glass eggs in the nests because the hens like to lay eggs in a nest with eggs in it. Leave the glass eggs in the nest," Mama instructed.

"Yes, I'll gather the eggs, Mama. It'll be fun. I'll be very careful not to break them."

Clarissa put on her apron, picked up the basket and went to the chicken coop. She opened the door and walked in. It was warm in the hen-house. Some of the hens were perched on the roosts, resting. A couple of hens were sitting in the nests on top of the eggs. Mama always reached under the sitting hen to gather eggs, but Clarissa was afraid to do that. Most of the hens were outside. One hen had just laid an egg and was cackling to announce her accomplishment.

Carefully, Clarissa reached in one of the nests and picked up some eggs. Then she went to another nest and gathered more eggs. Soon her basket was almost full. She opened the door and went outside. When she closed the door, she saw Mama talking to old Mr. Wheeler, the landlord.

The Adventures of Clarissa and Gregory

He sometimes came to check on his big red barn. Mama looked at the basket and smiled to see all the eggs Clarissa had gathered.

"Mama, I didn't break any of the eggs," Clarissa told her mother, proudly.

Mr. Wheeler said, "Someday Clarissa will grow up and get married and have a little girl of her own to gather eggs."

Clarissa listened and smiled. She thought that would be a very long time!

The End

Clarissa did grow up and get married, and had two daughters and a son of her own who she named Dawn, Rochelle and Bruce, but because they lived in a city, the children never got to gather eggs. When Dawn grew up and got married, her family moved to the country and raised chickens that laid eggs – so Dawn did indeed gather eggs!

How to make a Handkerchief Doll

1. Start with a square handkerchief (or any piece of fabric at least 8 x 8 inches — the larger the square, the easier it is to make the doll!)

2. Roll up the sides into the middle of the square

3. Flip it over

4. Fold the arms down

5. Tie the arms into a knot to make the head

6. Draw a face!

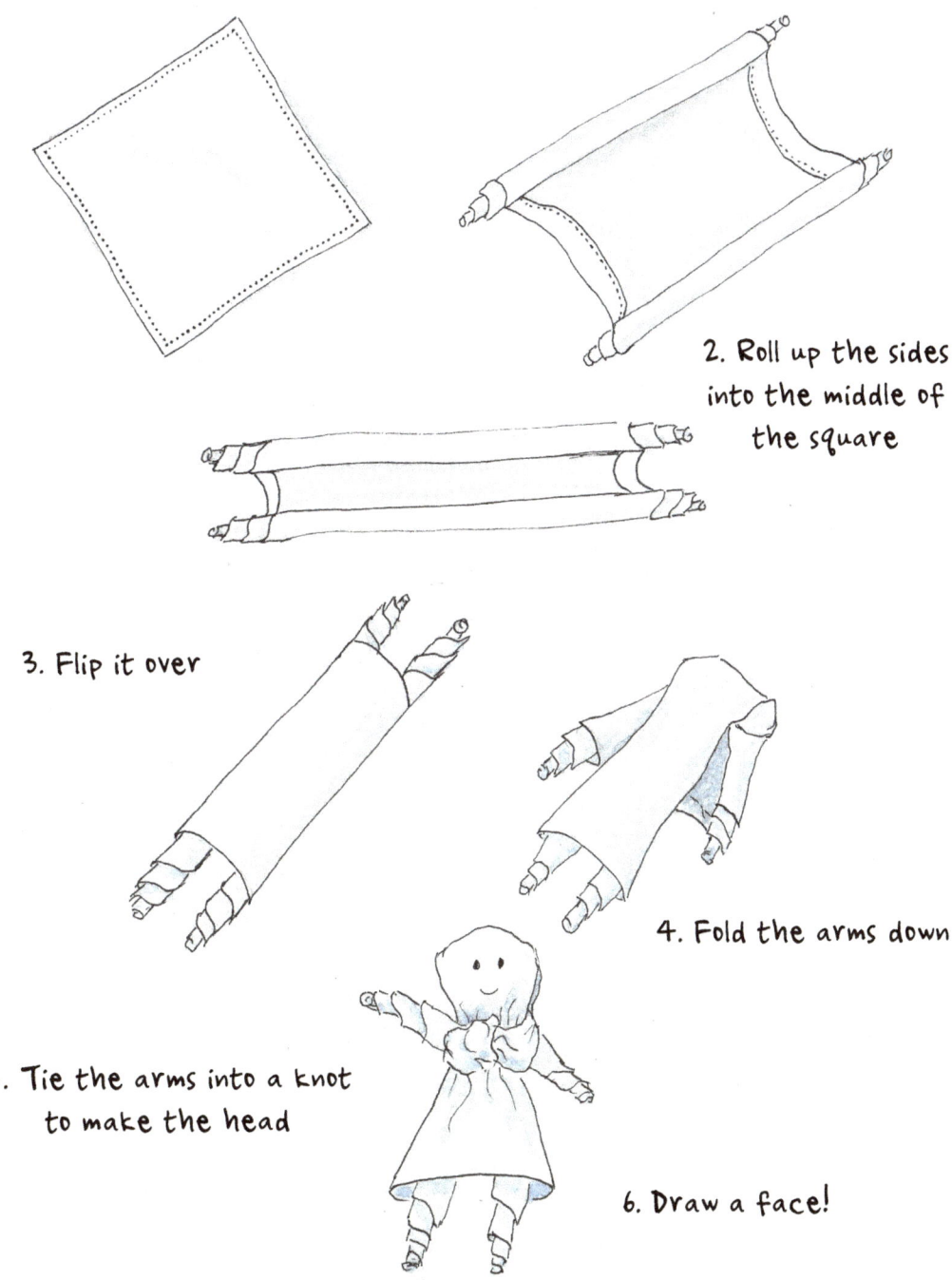

www.ingramcontent.com/pod-product-compliance
Lightning Source LLC
Chambersburg PA
CBHW051250110526

44588CB00025B/2945